sadonistic —
comic that pleasure is the principal
good &
would be the aim of action

10699607

WITHDRAWN
UTSA LIBRARIES

The Mother

Based on a novel by Gorky and set in Russia between 1905 and 1917, *The Mother* tells how an ordinary working-class woman is drawn by her son into the revolutionary movement. Though hostile at first and concerned only for her son's safety, she gradually becomes caught up in demonstrations, strike relief and the printing and distribution of illegal propaganda — teaching herself to read and getting herself beaten up into the bargain. The play is the often grim story of one woman's dawning political consciousness, but told by Brecht with all his customary irony and narrative drive.

Written in the very early 1930's during Brecht's most didactic phase, *The Mother* gains in warmth and humanity from its association with Helene Weigel and her magnificent portrayal of the central character in the play's first production in 1932, and again with the Berliner Ensemble in 1951. Her performance was immortalised on film in 1957.

This translation by Steve Gooch has been performed several times in Britain, most notably at the Half Moon Theatre, London, with Mary Sheen as the Mother in 1972 and again, by Belt and Braces, in 1977. For this edition he has recast the songs so they fit Hanns Eisler's original music for the play.

The photograph on the front cover shows Helene Weigel as the Mother in the opening scene of the 1951 production in Berlin. It is reproduced by courtesy of Foto Kiehl and the Berliner Ensemble. The photograph of Bertolt Brecht on the back cover is by Gerda Goedhart.

by the same author

in Methuen's Modern Plays

THE CAUCASIAN CHALK CIRCLE
THE DAYS OF THE COMMUNE
THE GOOD PERSON OF SZECHWAN
THE LIFE OF GALILEO
THE MEASURES TAKEN and other Lehrstücke
THE MESSINGKAUF DIALOGUES
MR PUNTILA AND HIS MAN MATTI
MOTHER COURAGE AND HER CHILDREN
THE RESISTIBLE RISE OF ARTURO UI
SAINT JOAN OF THE STOCKYARDS
THE THREEPENNY OPERA

in the Collected Works

COLLECTED PLAYS Volume 1 1918-1923
    (Baal, Drums in the Night, In the Jungle of the Cities,
    The Life of Edward II of England, and five one-act plays)
COLLECTED PLAYS Volume 7 1942-1946
    (The Visions of Simone Machard, Schweyk in the Second
    World War; The Caucasian Chalk Circle; The Duchess of Malfi)
POEMS 1913-1956

also available

BRECHT ON THEATRE

LIBRARY
The University of Texas
At San Antonio

Bertolt Brecht

THE MOTHER

Translated by Steve Gooch

EYRE METHUEN · LONDON

First published in Great Britain in 1978 by Eyre Methuen Ltd.
11 New Fetter Lane, London EC4P 4EE.
Published by arrangement with Suhrkamp Verlag, Frankfurt am
Main.

This translation copyright©Stefan Brecht 1978

Original work published under the title of DIE MUTTER
copyright 1957 by Suhrkamp Verlag Berlin.

Printed in Great Britain by
Whitstable Litho Ltd.

ISBN 0 413 38530 2

*This play is fully protected by copyright. All inquiries concerning
the rights for professional or amateur stage production should be
directed to the International Copyright Bureau Ltd, 26 Charing
Cross Road, London WC2.*

*This book is sold subject to the condition that it shall not, by
way of trade or otherwise, be lent, re-sold, hired out, or otherwise
circulated without the publisher's prior consent in any form of
binding or cover than that in which it is published and without a
similar condition including this condition being imposed on the
subsequent purchaser.*

Characters

Pelagea Vlasova
Pavel Vlasov
Anton
Andrei
Ivan
Mascha
Policeman
Commissioner
Factory porter
Smilgin
Karpov
Nikolai Vesovchikov
Sigorski
Prison warden
Lushin
Butcher
Vasil Yefimovitch
Butcher's wife
Workers, neighbours, strikebreakers, women.

Written 1930-31. Collaborators: Eisler, Weisenborn, Dudow.
First produced in Berlin at the Komödienhaus (Theater am
Schiffbauerdamm) on 17 January 1932, directed by Emil Burri,
scenery by Caspar Neher, with Helene Weigel as Vlasova and
Ernst Busch as Pavel.
Also produced by the Berliner Ensemble at Deutsches Theater,
Berlin, on 10 January 1951, directed by Brecht, scenery by
Neher, with Weigel as Vlasova.

1. VLASOVAS OF ALL COUNTRIES

Pelagea Vlasova's room in Tver.

VLASOVA: I'm almost ashamed to offer my son this soup. But
I can't put any more fat in it, not even half a spoonful.
Because only last week they took a kopeck per hour off his
wages, and I can't bring that back, whatever I do. I know, in a
long hard job like his he needs more substantial food. It's bad
I can't serve my only son up better soup; he's young and
virtually still growing. He's quite different from what his
father was. He's always reading books, and the food never was
good enough for him. Now the soup's got even worse. So he
just gets more and more discontented.

*She carries a tray with soup on it over to her son. When she gets
back, she watches as the son, without looking up from his book,
lifts the lid from the bowl, sniffs at the soup, then replaces the lid
and pushes the bowl away.*

Now he's turning his nose up at the soup again. I can't provide
him with any better. And soon he'll realise I'm no help to him
any more, just a burden. Why should I eat with him, live in his
room, clothe myself on his money? He'll go away, you'll see.
What can I, Pelagea Vlasova, a worker's widow and a worker's
mother, do? Every kopeck I turn over three times. I try it this
way, I try it that way. One day I'm scrimping on wood, the
next on clothes. But it's not enough. I don't see any answer.

The son, Pavel Vlasov, has taken his cap and the tray and gone.

CHORUS, *sung to Vlasova by the Revolutionary Workers*

Brush down that coat
Brush it twice over!
When you've finished brushing it
You're left with just a clean rag.

Cook too with care
Give it all you're able!
When your last kopeck's gone
Then your soup is just water.

Work at it, work at it more
Save up, make your money last
Budget, budget much better!

When your last kopeck's gone
There's nothing you can do.

> Whatever you do
> It won't be enough, though
> Your position is bad
> It'll get worse
> You can't go on this way
> And yet what is the answer?

Like the crow that no longer
Is able to feed its young
And defenceless against the winter blizzard
It can't see what to do and whines
You too can see no answer
And whine.

> Whatever you do
> It won't be enough, though
> Your position is bad
> It'll get worse
> You can't go on this way
> And yet what is the answer?

You work for no reward, no effort is too great
To replace the irreplaceable
Catching up with what can't be caught up with
When your last kopeck's gone, there is no work that's enough
Whether you get the meat that's missing from your kitchen
Will not be decided in the kitchen

> Whatever you do
> It won't be enough, though
> Your position is bad
> It'll get worse
> You can't go on this way
> And yet what is the answer?

2. PELAGEA VLASOVA IS DISTURBED TO SEE HER SON IN THE COMPANY OF REVOLUTIONARY WORKERS

Pelagea Vlasova's room.

Three workers and a young girl-worker arrive early in the morning with a duplicating machine.

ANTON: When you joined our movement two weeks ago, Pavel, you said we could come to your place if we had any special job to do. Your place is safest because we've never worked here before.

PAVEL: What do you want to do?

ANDREI: We've got to print today's leaflets. The latest wage cuts have really stirred the men up. For three days now we've been handing out leaflets at the factory. Today's the crucial day. Tonight the workers' assembly will decide whether we let them take a kopeck from us or whether we strike.

IVAN: We've brought the duplicator and some paper.

PAVEL: Sit down. My mother'll make us some tea.

They go over to the table.

IVAN *to Andrei*: You wait outside and keep an eye open for the police.

Andrei goes out.

ANTON: Where's Sidor?

MASCHA: My brother's not coming. On his way home last night he saw someone following him who looked like a policeman. So he thought he'd better go straight to the factory today.

PAVEL: Keep your voices down. It's best if my mother doesn't hear us. I haven't told her anything about all this up till now, she's no longer young enough and couldn't help us anyway.

ANTON: Here's the stencil.

They start working. One of them has hung a thick cloth in front of the window.

VLASOVA: I don't like seeing my son Pavel in these people's company. They'll end up taking him away from me completely. They're leading him on and getting him involved in something or the other. I'm not serving tea to people like that. *She goes up to the table.* Pavel, I can't make you any tea. There's not enough left. It won't make proper tea.

PAVEL: Then make us weak tea, Mother.

VLASOVA, *having gone back and sat down*: If I don't do as he says now, they'll realise I can't stand them. It doesn't suit me at all, them hanging round here, speaking soft so I can't hear anything. *She goes back to the table.* Pavel, it'd be very awkward for me, if the landlord noticed people getting together here at five o'clock in the morning and printing things. We can't pay the rent as it is.

IVAN: Believe me, Mrs Vlasova, we're concerned more about your rent than anything else. Basically we're concerned about nothing else, even if it doesn't look like it.

VLASOVA: I don't know so much.

She goes back.

ANTON: Your mother doesn't like us being here, Pavel?

IVAN: It's very difficult for your mother to understand that we've got to do what we're doing here, so that she can buy tea and pay the rent.

VLASOVA: Talk about thick-skinned! They just pretend not to have noticed anything. What are they up to with Pavel? He went to the factory and was glad to have a job. He didn't earn much, and this last year it's got less and less. If they take one more kopeck off him again now I'd sooner not eat myself. It worries me, though, the way he reads those books; and it bothers me, him running off to meetings of an evening, where things only get stirred up, instead of resting properly. All that'll do is lose him his job.

Mascha sings Vlasova the 'Song of the Answer'.

SONG OF THE ANSWER

> If you've not got any soup
> How can you stick up for yourself?
> That's when you must turn the whole state
> Upside down from top to bottom
> Till at last you've got your own soup.
> And then you will be your own guest.
>
> If there's not any work to be found for you
> Then you must stick up for yourself!
> That's when you must turn the whole state
> Upside down from top to bottom
> Till you find you are your own employer.
> And then there will be work on hand for you

When they laugh at you and say you're weak
You just can't afford to waste time.
That's when you must make quite sure that
All the weak march together.
And then you'll be a mighty force.
Whom no-one will laugh at again.

ANDREI, *comes in*: Police!

IVAN: Hide the paper!

Andrei takes the duplicator from Pavel and hangs it out of the window. Anton sits on the paper.

VLASOVA: You see, Pavel, now the police are coming. Pavel, what are you up to, what's on those leaflets?

MASCHA, *leads her over to the window and sits her on the divan*: You just sit there quietly, Mrs Vlasova.

A Policeman and a Commissioner come in.

POLICEMAN: Stay where you are! Anyone who moves will be shot! That's his mother, sir, and that's the man himself.

COMMISSIONER: Pavel Vlasov, I've a warrant to search these premises. What sort of smutty bunch is this you've dug up?

POLICEMAN: Sidor Khalatov's sister's here too — the man we arrested this morning. They're the ones all right.

MASCHA: What's happened to my brother?

COMMISSIONER: Your brother sends his best wishes. He's at our place now, revolutionising the bedbugs and enjoying a huge turnout. Only trouble is, he hasn't got any leaflets.

The workers look at each other.

We might just have a cell or two free still, next to his. You couldn't help me out with a few leaflets by any chance? Dear Mrs Vlasova, it's very much to my regret it should be your house in particular I have to come looking for leaflets in. *Goes over to the divan.* You see, Mrs Vlasova, now I'm forced for example, to open up your divan. You don't need that, do you? *He slits it open.*

PAVEL: No rouble notes in there, are there. That's because we're workers. We don't earn much.

COMMISSIONER: What about this mirror on the wall? Does it have to be smashed by the rude hand of a policeman? *He smashes it in*. You're a decent woman, Mrs Vlasova, I know that. And there was nothing in the divan either, that might have been construed as indecent. But what about this chest of drawers? A fine old piece. *He tips it over.* Well, well, look. Nothing behind that either, Mrs Vlasova, Mrs Vlasova! Honest people aren't cunning. Why should they be? And there's the dripping-pot, look, with its little spoon, the touching little dripping-pot. *He takes it from the shelf and drops it.* Now it's fallen on the floor, and now it turns out there's dripping in it.

PAVEL: Not very much. There's not much dripping in it. Commissioner. And there's not much bread in the bread-bin either, and not much tea in the caddy.

COMMISSIONER, *to the Policeman:* So it was a political dripping-pot after all. Mrs Vlasova, do you have to get mixed up with us bloodhounds in your age? Your curtains are washed so clean. You don't come across that often. It's a pleasure to look at them. *He rips them down.*

IVAN, *to Anton who has jumped up out of anxiety for the duplicator:* Don't move, they'll shoot you.

PAVEL, *loudly, to distract the Commissioner:* What's the point of chucking a pot of dripping on the floor?

ANDREI, *to the Policeman:* Pick that dripping-pot up!

POLICEMAN: That's Andrei Nakhodka, from Little Russia.

COMMISSIONER; *steps up to the table:* Andrei Maximovitch Nakhodka, you've been in police custody before for political activities, haven't you son?

ANDREI: Yes, in Rostov and Saratov. Only there the police called me 'sir'.

COMMISSIONER, *pulls a leaflet from his pocket:* Are you acquainted with the scum handing out these highly treasonable leaflets in the Suchlinov Works?

PAVEL: We're seeing scum here for the first time.

COMMISSIONER: You, Pavel Vlasov, are going to be taken down a peg or two. Sit down in a proper manner when I'm talking to you!

VLASOVA: Don't shout like that. You're a young man still. You've never known hardship. You're an official. You get a lot of money regularly for cutting open divans and looking to see there's no dripping in people's pots.

COMMISSIONER: You cry too soon, Mrs Vlasova. You'll be needing your tears later. You'd do better to keep an eye on your son. He's going the wrong way. *To the workers:* The day will come when even your cunning won't help you any more.

The Commissioner and the Policeman go. The workers clear up.

ANTON: Mrs Vlasova, we must ask you to forgive us. We didn't realise we were already under suspicion. Now your home's been smashed to pieces.

MASCHA: Are you very shaken, Mrs Vlasova?

VLASOVA: Yes. I can see Pavel's going the wrong way.

MASCHA: So you think it's right they can smash your home to pieces because your son's fighting for his kopeck?

VLASOVA: They're not doing right, but he's not doing right either.

IVAN, *back at the table*: What are we going to do now about handing out the leaflets?

ANTON: If we don't give the leaflets out today, everything we've said before is just hot air. The leaflets have got to be given out.

ANDREI: How many are there?

PAVEL: About five hundred.

IVAN: And who's giving them out?

ANTON: It's Pavel's turn today.

Vlasova beckons Ivan over to her.

VLASOVA: Who's supposed to be giving out the leaflets?

IVAN: Pavel. It's necessary.

VLASOVA: It's necessary! It starts with reading books and coming home late. Then there's these goings-on here in the house with machines like that, which you have to hang out the window. A cloth has to be hung up at the window. And all discussion has to be held in low voices. It's necessary! Then suddenly the police are in the house, and the policemen treat you like a criminal. *She stands.* Pavel, I forbid you to give out those leaflets.

ANDREI: It's necessary, Mrs Vlasova.

PAVEL, *to Mascha*: Tell her the leaflets have got to be given out for Sidor's sake, so he'll be cleared.

The workers go over to Vlasova. Pavel stays by the table.

MASCHA: Mrs Vlasova, it's necessary for my brother's sake too.

IVAN: Otherwise Siberia is all Sidor can look forward to.

ANDREI: If no more leaflets are given out today, they'll know for sure it must have been Sidor who gave them out yesterday.

ANTON: For that reason alone it's necessary to give out leaflets again today.

VLASOVA: I can see it's necessary to stop that young man you got into this being destroyed. But what'll happen to Pavel if he gets arrested?

ANTON: It's not that dangerous.

VLASOVA: I see, it's not that dangerous. A person's led astray and gets pulled in. To save him this and that is necessary. It's not dangerous, but it's necessary. We're under suspicion but we've got to give out leaflets. It's necessary, so it's not dangerous. And so it goes on. And at the end of it all a man stands by the gallows; put your head in the noose, it's not dangerous. Give me the leaflets. I'll go and hand them out, not Pavel.

ANTON: But how are you going to go about it?

VLASOVA: Don't you worry about that. I can bring it off as well as you can. My friend Maria Korsunova sells snacks at the factory in the lunch-hour. I'll do it for her today, and I'll wrap the food up in your leaflets. *She goes and fetches her shopping-bag.*

MASCHA: Pavel, your mother's offered to hand out the leaflets for us herself.

PAVEL: Think over what's for it and against it, I ask you, though not to have me voice an opinion on my mother's offer.

ANTON: Andrei?

ANDREI: I think she can do it. She's known amongst the workers and she won't be suspected by the police.

ANTON: Ivan?

IVAN: I think so too.

ANTON: Even if she's caught, less can happen to her. She doesn't belong to the movement and she'll have done it solely for her

son's sake. Comrade Vlasov, in view of the urgency of the
situation and the extreme danger to Comrade Sidor, we're in
favour of accepting your mother's offer.

IVAN: We're convinced she runs the least risk.

PAVEL: It's all right by me.

VLASOVA, *to herself*: I'm definitely helping out in a bad cause
here, but I've got to keep Pavel out of it.

ANTON: Mrs Vlasova, we'll hand this packet of leaflets over to
you, then.

ANDREI: So now you're fighting for us, Pelagea Vlasova.

VALSOVA: Fighting? I'm not a young woman any more and I'm
no fighter. I'm happy just to scrape my few kopecks together.
That's enough of a fight for me.

ANDREI: D'you know what's in the leaflets, Mrs Vlasova ?

VLASOVA: No, I can't read.

3. THE SWAMP KOPECK

Factory yard.

VLASOVA, *with a large basket, in front of the factory gates*: It all
depends what kind of man the porter is. Whether he's lazy or
particular. All I've got to do is persuade him to issue me with a
pass. Then I can wrap the food in the leaflets. If they catch me
I'll just say: someone planted them on me, I can't read. *She
observes the factory porter.* He's fat and lazy. I'll see what he
does when I offer him a pickled onion. His kind like their food
and never have a penny.

She goes up to the gates and drops a parcel in front of the porter.

Here, you, I've dropped one of my parcels.

The porter looks the other way.

Well fancy that. I completely forgot I only need to put the
basket down and then I've got my hands free. And there I was,
nearly troubling you. *To the audience*: The hard-boiled type,
this one. You've got to come the old flannel with him, then

he'll do anything, just for peace and quiet's sake. *She goes up to the entrance and speaks quickly.* That's just typical of Maria Korsunova. I said to her only the day before yesterday: whatever you do, don't get wet feet. But d'you think she listened to me? No. She goes out digging potatoes again and gets wet feet. Next morning she's feeding the goats. Wet feet! What about that, eh? Next thing, of course, she's on her back. Only instead of staying put in bed, she's off out again in the evening. It rains of course, so what does she get? Wet feet.

PORTER: You can't come in here without a pass.

VLASOVA: That's what I told her. You know, we're as thick as thieves us two, but talk about obstinate, you've never seen the like. Vlasova, I'm ill, you've got to go to the factory and sell my food. You see, Maria, I said, now you've got a sore throat. But why have you got a sore throat? You just throw those wet feet in my face once more, she says — and all this in a voice more'n a croak — and I'll chuck this cup at that big head of yours! Talk about obstinate!

The porter sighs and lets her through.

Quite right, I'm only holding you up.

It's the lunch-hour. The workers sit on crates, etc. and eat. Vlasova offers her wares. Ivan Vesovchikov helps her wrap them up.

VLASOVA: Pickled onions, tobacco, tea, fresh pies!

IVAN: And the wrapping-paper's the best part.

VLASOVA: Pickled onions, tobacco, tea, fresh pies!

IVAN: And the wrapping-paper's free.

A WORKER: Got a pickled onion?

VLASOVA: Yes, pickled onions here.

IVAN: And don't throw the wrapping-paper away.

VLASOVA: Pickled onions, tobacco, tea, hot pies!

A WORKER: Here, anything interesting in the wrapping-paper today? I can't read.

ANOTHER WORKER: How should I know what your wrapping-paper says?

1ST WORKER: Come on, mate, you've got the same thing in your hand.

2ND WORKER: You're right. There's something on it.

1ST WORKER: What, though?

SMILGIN, *an old worker*: I'm against leaflets like this being given out while negotiation's still going on.

2ND WORKER: They're quite right. Once we let ourselves in for negotiation, we're up shit creek.

VLASOVA, *across the yard*: Pickled onions, tobacco, tea, fresh pies!

3RD WORKER: They got the police on their backs, control on the factory gate's been sharpened up, and still another leaflet turns up. They know what they're doing these blokes, and they won't be stopped. There's something in what they're after.

1ST WORKER: Yeah, I got to say myself, when I see something like this, I'm all for it.

PAVEL: Here comes Karpov at long last.

ANTON: I wonder how far he's got.

KARPOV, *comes in*: Are all the shop stewards here?

In one corner of the factory-yard the shop-stewards of the factory gather together. Amongst them Smilgin, Anton and Pavel.

Brothers, we have negotiated!

ANTON: How far d'you get?

KARPOV: Brothers, it is not without some succes we return to you.

ANTON: D'you get the kopeck?

KARPOV: Brothers, we put our calculations to Mr Suchlinov. The deduction of a kopeck per hour from the wages of 800 workers comes to 24,000 roubles a year. These 24,000 roubles would, from now on, have flowed into the pocket of Mr Suchlinov. This had to be avoided at all costs. Now, after a struggle lasting four hours, we've got there. We avoided it. Those 24,000 roubles will not flow into Mr Suchlinov's pocket.

ANTON: So you got the kopeck?

KARPOV: Brothers, it has always been our contention that the factory's sanitary conditions are intolerable.

PAVEL: D'you get the kopeck, though?

KARPOV: The swamp outside the East Gate of the factory has always been a basic menace.

ANTON: Ah I see, You want to get round it with the swamp!

KARPOV: Remember the clouds of flies that make it impossible
for us to spend any time in the fresh air every summer; the high
sickness rate from swamp-fever; the constant threat to our children.
Brothers, for 24,000 roubles the swamp can be dried out. And that
Mr Suchlinov is prepared to do. Enlargement of the factory would
then be set in the motion on the reclaimed land. That'll provide
more jobs. As you well know, what's good for the factory is also
good for you. Brothers, the factory is not doing as well as we
may perhaps believe. We cannot conceal from you what Mr
Suchlinov has communicated to us: our sister-factory in Tver is
being closed down, and as from tomorrow 700 colleagues will
be out on the street. We are in favour of the lesser evil. Every
man of unclouded vision must realise with sorrow that we stand
on the brink of one of the greatest economic crises our country
has ever known.

ANTON: So capitalism's sick, and you're the doctor. Are you
saying you're in favour of accepting the wage cut?

KARPOV: We could find no other solution in the course of our
negotiations.

ANTON: In that case we demand that negotiation with the
management be broken off. You couldn't stop the wage cut, and
we reject the swamp kopeck.

KARPOV: I must warn you not to break off negotiation with the
management.

SMILGIN: You have to realise this means a strike.

ANTON: In our view only a strike can save our kopeck.

IVAN: The question before this meeting today is quite simply this:
should Mr Suchlinov's swamp be dried out, or should our kopeck
be saved? We must go ahead with our strike, and by the first of
May, which is only a week off, we must try to effect the shut-
down of all other factories where wages are to be cut.

KARPOV: I'm warning you!

*The factory siren. The workers stand up to go back to work. They
sing the "Song of the Patch and the Coat" back over their
shoulders to Karpov and Smilgin.*

SONG OF THE PATCH AND THE COAT

> Every time that our coat's in tatters

Then you come running and say: this won't do at all
It must be put right this minute, we'll use all our powers!
Full of fervour you run to the bosses
While we stand here freezing, waiting.
Until you come back and show in triumph
What it is you've brought us from your conquest:
Just a little patch.

> Fine, you've got a patch
> But where's the rest
> The coat itself?

Every time we cry out in hunger
Then you come running and say: this won't do at all
It must be put right this minute, we'll use all our powers!
Full of fervour you run to the bosses
While we stand here hungry, waiting.
Until you come back and show in triumph
What it is you've brought us from your conquest:
A slice of bread.

> Fine, you've got the slice
> But where's the rest
> The loaf itself?

We need a bit more than patches
We need the whole coat itself.
We need a bit more than slices
We need the whole loaf itself.
We don't just need a mere job to do
We now need the whole factory.
And the coalmines and the ore
And power in the state.

> So, that is what we're asking
> But what is
> Offered us instead?

The workers, except for Karpov and Smilgin go off.

KARPOV: All right then, strike! *He goes off.*

Vlasova comes back and sits down, counting her takings,

SMILGIN, *with a leaflet in his hand*: So it's you handing these out. Do you realise these pieces of paper mean a strike?

VLASOVA: A strike? How come?

SMILGIN: These leaflets call on the employees of the Suchlinov plant to strike.

VLASOVA: I don't understand any of that.

SMILGIN: Why are you giving them out then?

VLASOVA: We've got our reasons all right. Why are they arresting our people?

SMILGIN: Have you got any idea what's on these things?

VLASOVA: No, I can't read.

SMILGIN: This is how our people get stirred up. A strike's a nasty business. Tomorrow morning they won't be going to work. But what'll happen tomorrow evening? And what'll happen next week? It makes no difference to the firm whether we go on working or not. But for us it's life itself. *The factory policeman comes running up with the porter.* Anton Antonovitch, are you looking for something?

PORTER: Yes, leaflets have been handed out again, calling for a strike. I don't know how they've been getting in. What's that you've got there?

Smilgin tries to hide his leaflet in his pocket.

POLICEMAN: What's that you're sticking in your pocket? *He pulls it out.* A leaflet!

PORTER: Do you read those leaflets, Smilgin?

SMILGIN: Anton Antonovitch, my friend, surely we're allowed to read what we want.

POLICEMAN: Oh Yes? *He grabs him by the collar and drags him along with him.* I'll show you what it means to read leaflets calling for a strike in your factory!

SMILGIN: I'm against the strike. Karpov can bear me out.

POLICEMAN: Tell me where you got that leaflet then.

SMILGIN, *after a pause*: It was lying on the ground.

POLICEMAN, *hits him:* I'll give you leaflets!

The factory policeman and the porter go off with Smilgin.

VLASOVA: All the man did, though, was buy a pickled onion!

4. PELAGEA VLASOVA IS GIVEN HER FIRST LESSON IN ECONOMICS

Pelagea Vlasova's room.

VLASOVA: Pavel, on your behalf I gave out the leaflets you people gave me today to avert suspicion from the young man you'd got into all this. When I'd finished giving them out, I had to look on while another man, who'd done nothing but read that leaflet was arrested in front of my eyes. What have you made me do?

ANTON: Mrs Vlasova, we thank you for your skilful work.

VLASOVA: So you call that skilful do you? But what about Smilgin, who I've put in prison with my skilfulness?

ANDREI: You didn't put him in prison. To our mind it was the police who put him in prison.

IVAN: He was let free again, because they had to admit he was one of the few who spoke against the strike. Now, though, he's for the strike. Mrs Vlasova, you've been instrumental in uniting the workers at the Suchlinov plant. As you must have heard, the strike has been almost unanimously agreed on.

VLASOVA: I didn't want to cause a strike. I wanted to help a man. Why do people get arrested for reading leaflets? What did it say in that leaflet?

MASCHA: When you handed it out you were giving good help to a good cause.

VLASOVA: What did it say in that leaflet?

PAVEL: What do you think it said?

VLASOVA: Something wrong.

ANTON: Mrs. Vlasova, we realise we owe you an explanation.

PAVEL: Sit down with us, Mother, we want to explain it to you.

They lay a cloth over the divan. Ivan hangs a new mirror on the wall. Mascha puts a new dripping pot on the table. Then they fetch themselves chairs and sit down around Vlasova.

IVAN: You see, in the leaflet it said we workers shouldn't put up with Mr Suchlinov cutting the wages he pays us as and when he pleases.

VLASOVA: Nonsense, what are you going to do to stop him? Why shouldn't Mr Suchlinov be able to cut the wages he pays you as and when he pleases? Does his factory belong to him or doesn't it?

PAVEL: It belongs to him.

VLASOVA: Right then. This table, for example, belongs to me. Now I'll ask you a question: can I do what I like with this table?

ANDREI: Yes, Mrs Vlasova. You can do what you like with it.

VLASOVA: Right then. Can I, for example, smash it to pieces if I like?

ANTON: Yes, you can smash it to pieces if you like.

VLASOVA: Aha! In that case Mr Suchlinov, whose factory belongs to him just as my table does to me, can do what he likes with it.

PAVEL: No.

VLASOVA: Why not?

PAVEL: Because he needs us workers for his factory.

VLASOVA: But what if he says he doesn't need you anymore?

IVAN: Look, Mrs Vlasova, look at it this way: some days he needs us some days he doesn't.

ANTON: Right.

IVAN: When he needs us, we have to be there. When he doesn't need us we're still there. Where else can we go? And he knows that. He doesn't always need us, but we always need him. He counts on that. Mr Suchlinov has got his machines standing there, all right. But those are our tools. We haven't got any others. We haven't got any other looms or lathes for the very reason it's Mr Suchlinov's machines we use. His factory belongs to him, but when he shuts it, he takes our tools away.

VLASOVA: Because your tools belong to him the way my table does to me.

ANTON: Yes, but do you think it's right our tools belong to him?

VLASOVA, *loudly*: No! But whether I think it's right or whether I don't, they still belong to him, don't they? Somebody could just as well not think it right my table belongs to me.

ANDREI: Then we say, there's a difference between owning a table and owning a factory.

MASCHA: Of course a table can belong to you, a chair too. That

doesn't hurt anybody, does it. Even if you put it on the roof, wha
harm can it do? If you own a factory, though, you can hurt
many hundreds of people.

IVAN: Because you have their tools in your possession, and that
way you can use people.

VLASOVA: Yes all right, he can use us. Don't treat me as if I
hadn't noticed that over the last forty years. There's only one
thing I haven't noticed, though, and that is that there's
anything you can do about it.

ANTON: Mrs Vlasova, we've now reached the point in talking
about Mr Suchlinov's property where we've esbatlished that his
factory is property of a totally different kind from, say, your
table. He can use his property to use us.

IVAN: And his property has yet another unusual property: unless
he uses us with it, it's absolutely worthless to him. Only as
long as it's our tool is it worth anything to him. When it's no
longer our means of production, it's a heap of old iron. So he's
also dependent on us with his property.

VLASOVA: All right. But how are you going to prove to him
that he's dependent on you?

ANDREI: Look: if he, Pavel, Vlasov, goes up to Mr Suchlinov and
says: Mr Suchlinov, without me your factory is a heap of old
iron, so you can't knock my wages down as and when you
please, Mr Suchlinov will laugh and throw Vlasov out. But when
all the Vlasovs in Tver, eight hundred Vlasovs, stand there and say
the same thing, Mr Suchlinov won't be laughing any more.

VLASOVA: And that's what your strike is?

PAVEL: Yes, that's what our strike is.

VLASOVA: And that's what it said in that leaflet?

PAVEL: Yes, that's what it said in that leaflet.

VLASOVA: A strike's a nasty business. What am I supposed to
cook with? What's going to happen about the rent? You won't
be going to work tomorrow morning, but what about next week?
All right, though, we'll get round that somehow too. But if it
only said all that about the strike, why'd the police arrest people?
What's the police got to do with it?

PAVEL: Well, mother, that's what we're asking you: what have the
police got to do with it?

VLASOVA: If we carry out our strike with Mr Suchlinov, it's got nothing to do with the police. You must've gone about it in the wrong way. Misunderstandings occurred, I expect. People thought you were up to something violent. What you should have done is show the whole town your quarrel with the management is a just and peaceful one. That'd make a big impression.

IVAN: That's exactly what we intend to do, Mrs Vlasova. On the first of May, the international day workers' struggle, when all the factories in Tver will be demonstrating for the liberation of the working class, we will carry banners calling on all factories in Tver to support our fight for the kopeck.

VLASOVA: If you march peacefully through the streets and only carry your banners, no one can object to that.

ANDREI: We're assuming Mr Suchlinov won't stand for it.

VLASOVA: Well, he's got to stand for it.

IVAN: The police will probably break the demonstration up.

VLASOVA: What's the police got to do with this Suchlinov? I mean, the police watch over us, yes, but they watch over Mr Suchlinov just as much.

PAVEL: So you think the police'll take no action against a peaceful demonstration, do you mother?

VLASOVA: Yes I do. There's nothing violent in it after all. We'd never agree on anything violent. You know I believe in a God in heaven. I don't want anything to do with violence. I've got to know it over the past forty years, and I've never been able to do anything against it. But when I die, I should like, at least not to have done anything violent.

5. REPORT ON THE 1ST MAY, 1905

Street.

PAVEL: As we, the workers from the Suchlinov plant, crossed over the Wool Market, we met the column from the other factories. There were already many thousands of us. We carried banners saying: 'Workers, support our fight against the wage cut! Workers, unite!'

IVAN: We marched in a quiet and orderly fashion. Songs like 'Arise, ye prisoners of starvation' and Comrades, the bugles are sounding' were sung. Our factory marched immediately behind the great red flag.

ANDREI: Beside me, close behind her son, marched Pelagea Vlasova. When we'd gone round early that morning to pick him up, she suddenly came out of the kitchen, dressed to go out. And when we asked where she was going, she answered.

VLASOVA: With you.

ANTON: Many like her went with us. The harsh winter, the wage cuts in the factories and our agitation had led many to us. Before we arrived at the Boulevard of Our Saviour we saw only a few policemen and no soldiers, but on the corner of the Boulevard of Our Saviour and the Tverskaya there suddenly stood a double chain of soldiers. When they saw our flag and our banners, a voice suddenly called out to us 'Attention! Disperse immediately! We have orders to shoot!' And : Drop your flag.' Our column came to a halt.

PAVEL: But because the ones marching at the back were still moving forward, the ones at the front couldn't stop, and so they opened fire. As the first people turned, what followed was nothing but confusion. Many couldn't believe that what they saw had actually happened. Then the soldiers started to move towards the crowd.

VLASOVA: I went along to demonstrate for the workers' cause. The people marching there were all quite orderly people who'd worked their whole lives. Of course there were desperate ones amongst them too, people driven by unemployment to extremes, and hungry people too weak to defend themselves.

ANDREI: We were still standing quite near the front, and we still didn't break up when they opened fire.

PAVEL: We had our flag. Smilgin was carrying it, and we had no intention whatsoever of giving it away, for it seemed to us then, without consulting each other in any way, that it was important it should be us in particular they hit and threw down and our flag in particular, the red flag, they took away. The reason we wanted that, though, was so that all workers would see who we were and who we were for, namely the workers.

ANDREI: Those who were against us had to behave like wild animals. That was what they received their livelihood from the Suchlinovs for.

MASCHA: In the end everyone would see it, and our flag, the red flag, had to be held especially high, so that everyone could see it, not least the soldiers, but everyone else too.

IVAN: And for those who didn't see it, to them it would have to be told today, tomorrow or in the years to come, as long as it took for it to be seen again. For we felt we knew, and many came to know for sure at that moment, that it would be seen again and again from now on until everything we were marching against had changed completely. Our flag, which is the most dangerous for all exploiters and rulers, the most relentless!

ANTON: But for us workers, supreme!

EVERYONE: That's why you will always see it
Over and over
Gladly or sadly
Depending where you stand in this fight
Which can end in no other way
Than victory once and for all
For the sore oppressed of every nation.

VLASOVA: But on that day it was Smilgin, the worker, who carried it.

SMILGIN: My name is Smilgin. I've belonged to the movement twenty years. I was one of the first to spread revolutionary consciousness in the factory. We fought for our wages and for better working conditions. During which, in my colleagues' interest, I often had dealings with the management. To begin with full of antagonism, but then, I must admit, I thought it might be easier the other way. If we widened our influence, I thought, we would get a say in things. That was wrong, of course. I'm standing here now, behind me there are already many thousands, but once again power blocks our path. Should we give up the flag?

ANTON: Don't give it up, Smilgin. Bargaining won't work, we said. And Pelagea Vlasova told him:

VLASOVA: You mustn't give it up. Nothing can happen to you. The police can't object to a peaceful demonstration.

MASCHA: At that moment an officer called out to us: 'Hand over your flag!'

IVAN: And Smilgin looked back and saw our banners behind his flag; and on those banners, our demands. And behind the banners stood the strikers from the Suchlinov plant. And we watched what he, one of us, standing beside us, would do with the flag.

PAVEL: Twenty years in the movement, worker, revolutionary, on the first of May 1905, 11 o'clock in the morning on the corner of the Boulevard of Our Saviour, at the decisive moment. He said:

SMILGIN: I will not hand it over ! There will be no negotiation!

ANDREI: Good, Smilgin, we said. That's right. Now everything's straight.

IVAN: Yes, he said and pitched forward on his face, for they'd shot him down.

ANDREI: And then they ran up, four, five men, to pick up the flag. But the flag lay beside him. So our Pelagea Vlasova bent down the quiet, even-tempered one, the comrade, and picked up the flag.

VLASOVA: Give me the flag, Smilgin, I said. Give it here. I'll carry it. All this is going to be changed!

6. THE TEACHER VESOVCHIKOV'S FLAT IN ROSTOV.

a. After the arrest of her son, Pelagea Vlasova is taken by Ivan Vesovchikov to his brother, Nikolai, the teacher.

IVAN: Nikolai Ivanovitch, I've brought you our friend Pavel's mother, Pelagea Vlasova. Her son was arrested because of what happened at the demonstration on the first of May. Since then she's been served notice to leave her old flat, and we promised her son we'd see her safe. Your flat isn't under suspicion. No one can claim you have anything at all to do with the revolutionary movement.

VESOVCHIKOV: Certainly, that is only too true. I'm a teacher, I'd lose my job if I started pursuing the kind of wild fancies you do.

IVAN: Anyway, I hope you'll keep Mrs Vlasova on here all the same. She's got nowhere else to go. You'd be doing your brother a great favour.

VESOVCHIKOV: I've got no reason to do you a favour. I disapprove of everything you do in the extreme, It's all nonsense. I've proved that to you often enough. But that doesn't apply to you, Mrs Vlasova. I can well appreciate your plight. Besides I'm in need of a housekeeper anyway. As you can see, this place is terribly untidy.

IVAN: You'll have to give her some money for her work of course. She has to send her son a bit now and then.

VESOVCHIKOV: I could only offer you a very small allowance, naturally.

IVAN: He knows as much about politics as that chair, but he's not inhuman.

VESOVCHIKOV: You're an idiot, Ivan. Mrs Vlasova, there's a sofa in the kitchen. You can sleep on there. I see you've brought your own linen. The kitchen's this way, Mrs. Vlasova.

Pelagea Vlasova takes her bundle into the kitchen and starts installing herself there.

IVAN: I thank you, Nikolai Ivanovitch, and ask you to watch over her. She mustn't have anything to do with politics again just yet. She got involved in the first of May distrubances and ought to take it easy for a while. She's very concerned about what will happen to her son. I'll hold you responsible for her.

VESOVCHIKOV: I shan't draw her into politics, the way you people do.

b. The teacher Vesovchikov catches his housekeeper at her agitation work.

Neighbours sit in the kitchen around Pelagea Vlasova.

WOMAN: We heard communism was a crime, though.

VLASOVA: That's not true. Communism's good for people like us. What can be said against it? *she sings*

IN PRAISE OF COMMUNISM

It's quite straightforward, you'll understand it. It's not hard.
Because you're not an exploiter, you'll quickly grasp it.
It's for your good, so find out all about it.
They're fools who describe it as foolish, and foul who describe
it as foulness.
It's against all that's foul and against all that's foolish.
The exploiters will tell you that it's criminal
But we know better:
It puts an end to all that's criminal.
It isn't madness, but puts
An end to all madness.
It doesn't mean chaos
It just means order.
It's just the simple thing
That's hard, so hard to do.

WOMAN: Why don't all workers see that, though?

SIGORSKI, *quotes*: 'Because they are kept in ignorance of their
being exploited, of this being a crime, and of it being possible
to put an end to this crime.'

They fall silent. Vesovchikov has come into the next room.

VESOVCHIKOV: I come home tired from the public house, my
head still full of debates during which I once again got very
angry with that idiot Sachar, who kept on contradicting me,
although I was, of course, in the right, and now I'm looking
forward to the peace and quiet of my own four walls. I think
I'll just bathe my feet and read the paper while doing so.

VLASOVA, *comes in*: Oh, you're back early, Nikolai Ivanovitch?

VESOVCHIKOV: Yes, and I'd like you to prepare me a hot foot-
bath, please. I'll take it in the kitchen.

VLASOVA: It's good that you've come, Nikolai Ivanovitch, very
good, because you've got to go out again straight away. The
lady next door told me just this minute that your friend Sachar
Smerdyakov was here an hour ago. He couldn't leave a
message, though, as he had to speak to you urgently in person.

VESOVCHIKOV: Mrs Vlasova, I've been with my friend Sachar
Smerdyakov the whole evening.

VLASOVA: Really? But the kitchen's a mess, Nikolai Ivanovitch.
The washing's hanging up.

Murmurs from the kitchen.

VESOVCHIKOV: Since when has my washing talked while it's drying, and − *He points to the samovar she's holding* − since when have my shirts drunk tea?

VLASOVA: Nikolai Ivanovitch, I must confess to you, I've invited some friends for tea, to sit and talk.

VESOVCHIKOV: I see. What kind of people are they?

VLASOVA: I don't know if you'll feel at ease with them, Nikolai Ivanovitch. They're not particularly well-off as people.

VESOVCHIKOV: Aha, so you're talking politics again! Is that unemployed chap, Sigorski, with them?

VLASOVA: Yes. And his wife and his brother with his son and his uncle and his aunt. They're very intelligent people. I'm sure even you would follow their arguments with interest.

VESOVCHIKOV: Mrs Vlasova, have I not already made it clear to you that I don't want anything political in this house? Now I come home tired from my local and find my kitchen full of politics. I'm surprised, Mrs Vlasova, I'm very surprised.

VLASOVA: Nikolai Ivanovitch, I'm sorry I've had to let you down. I was telling the people about the first of May. They didn't know enough about it.

VESOVCHIKOV: What do you know of politics, Mrs Vlasova? Only this evening I was saying to my friend Sachar, a very intelligent man: 'Sachar Smerdyakov, there is nothing on earth more difficult and more impenetrable than politics.'

VLASOVA: You must be very tired and tense, Nikolai Ivanovitch. But if you had a little time to spare − we were all agreed this evening that you might be able to explain a lot to us, even concerning the first of May, which is a very impenetrable subject.

VESOVCHIKOV: I may say I have little desire to argue the toss with the redundant Mr Sigorski. At best I might try to educate them in the fundamentals of politics. But really, Mrs Vlasova, I have grave misgivings, finding you in the company of such dubious individuals. Bring the samovar in and some bread and a few pickled onions.

They go into the kitchen.

c. Pelagea Vlasova learns to read

VESOVCHIKOV, *in front of a blackboard*: So you want to learn t
read. I don't understand of course why you people should need
it in your position. Some of you are also a little old for it.
However, I shall try, as a favour to Mrs Vlasova. Do you all have
something to write with? Right, I shall now write three simple
words up: sap, nest, fish. I repeat: sap, nest, fish. *He writes*.

SIGORSKI: Why words like that?

VLASOVA, *sitting at the table with the others*: Excuse me, Nikola
Ivanovitch, does it absolutely have to be sap, nest, fish? We're o
people. We've got to learn the words we need quickly, you knov

VESOVCHIKOV, *smiles*: But you see, *what* you learn to read by is
completely irrelevant.

VLASOVA: What do you mean? How'd you spell 'worker' for
instance? That's what interests our Pavel Sigorski.

SIGORSKI: 'Sap' never comes up at all.

VLASOVA: He's a metal-worker.

VESOVCHIKOV: The letters come up in it, though.

WORKER: But the letters come up in the word 'class-struggle' too!

VESOVCHIKOV: Yes, but you've got to start off with what's
simplest, not tackle the most difficult straight away. 'Sap' is
simple.

SIGORSKI: 'Class-struggle' is a lot simpler.

VESOVCHIKOV: But there's no such thing as class-struggle. We
ought to get that straight from the start.

SIGORSKI, *stands up*: In that case, if you think there's no class-
struggle, there's nothing I can learn from you.

VLASOVA: You're here to learn reading and writing, and you can
do that here. Reading is class-struggle.

VESOVCHIKOV: All this is nonsense in my opinion. What's that
supposed to mean anyway: reading is class-struggle? Why are
you talking like this in the first place? *He writes*. Right then,
here we have: worker. Copy it.

VLASOVA: Reading is class-struggle. What I meant by that was, if
the soldiers in Tver had been able to read our banners, perhaps
they wouldn't have shot at us. They were all peasant boys.

VESOVCHIKOV: Look here, I'm a teacher myself, and I've been teaching reading and writing eighteen years, but I'll tell you something. Deep inside me I know it's all nonsense. Books are nonsense. Men are only made worse by them. A simple peasant is a better human being for that reason alone, that he hasn't been spoiled by civilisation.

VLASOVA: So how d'you spell 'class-struggle'? Pavel Sigorski, you have to hold your hand firmly or it'll shake and your writing won't be clear.

VESOVCHIKOV, *writes*: Class-struggle. *To Sigorski*: You must write in a straight line and not go over the margin. He who trangresses the margin also trangresses the law. Generation after generation after all has heaped knowledge upon knowledge and written book after book. Science has advanced further than ever before. And what use has it been? Confusion too is greater than ever before. The whole lot ought to be thrown in the sea at its deepest point. Every book and machine in the Black Sea. Down with knowledge! Have you finished yet? I sometimes have lessons in which I sink into total melancholy. What, I ask then, what have such truly great thoughts, which encompass not only the Now, but also the Ever and Eternal, Human Nature, what have they to do with class-struggle?

SIGORSKI, *muttering*: Thoughts like that are no use to us. As long as your kind are sinking in melancholy, you're exploiting us.

VLASOVA: Quiet, Pavel Sigorski! Please, how d'you spell 'exploitation'?

VESOVCHIKOV: 'Exploitation'! That only exists in books too. As if I'd ever exploited anyone! *He writes*.

SIGORSKI: He only says that cos he doesn't see any of the profits.

VLASOVA, *to Sigorski*: The 'o' in 'exploitation' is just like the 'o' in 'worker'.

VESOVCHIKOV: Knowledge doesn't help, you know. It's kindness that helps.

VLASOVA: You give us your knowledge then, if you don't need it.

IN PRAISE OF LEARNING, *sung by the Revolutionary workers to those who are learning*

> Learn what is easiest, for all
> Those whose day has come at last
> It is not too late!

Learn up your ABC, it is not enough but
Learn it! Don't let it overawe you
Start now! You must omit nothing!
It's you who'll have to give the orders.

Learn on, man put away!
Learn on, man put in prison!
Learn on, woman in kitchen!
Learn on, old age pensioner!
It's you who'll have to give the orders
Go off and find a school, if you're homeless!
Go get yourself knowledge, you who freeze!
Starving, you reach for the book: it is your best weapon.
It's you who'll have to give the orders.

Don't be afraid to ask questions, comrade!
Don't be talked into things
See for yourself!
What you don't know yourself
You don't know.
Study the bill for
It's you who must pay it.
Point with your finger at every item
Ask how it comes to be there.
It's you who'll have to give the orders.

VLASOVA, *stands up*: That's enough for taday. We can't take all
that much in at once any more. Otherwise our Pavel Sigorski
won't get any sleep again tonight. Thank you, Nikolai Ivanovitch.
We can only say you help us a lot by teaching us reading and
writing.

VESOVCHIKOV: I don't believe it. By the way, I don't say your
opinions don't make sense. I shall come back to that in our
next lesson.

d. Ivan Vesovchikov doesn't recognise his brother anymore.

IVAN: The comrades here in Rostov have spoken to me about
your work, Pelagea Nilovna — about your mistakes too. They've
asked me to pass something on to you: your party card.

VLASOVA: Thank you. *She receives it.*

IVAN: Has Pavel written to you?

VLASOVA: No. I'm very worried about him. The worst thing is, I never know at any moment what he's doing or what they're doing to him. I don't even know for example if they're giving him enough food or if he's not getting cold perhaps. Do they get blankets there in fact?

IVAN: There were blankets in Odessa.

VLASOVA: I'm very proud of him. I'm lucky. I have a son who's needed. *She recites.*

IN PRAISE OF THE REVOLUTIONARY

> Many are too much.
> When they've gone, it's for the better
> But when he's not there we miss him.
>
> When oppression increases
> Many get discouraged
> But his courage grows.
>
> He's ready to organise, fight
> For a wage rise, to strike for a tea break and
> Fight for power in the state.
>
> He asks of property:
> Where d'you come from?
> He asks of factions
> Whom do you serve?
>
> Where things always get hushed up
> He'll ask awkward questions
> And where the oppressors rule and there's those who blame
> fate for it
> That's when he'll name the guilty.
>
> Where he sits at table
> Dissatisfaction also sits at table.
> Food becomes bad
> And it's seen that the room is tiny.
>
> Wherever they chase him, with him
> Goes rebellion, and where he is banished
> Discontent stays behind.

VESOVCHIKOV, *comes in*: Good day, Ivan.

IVAN: Good day, Nikolai.

VESOVCHIKOV: I'm glad to see you're still a free man.

IVAN: I just wanted to look in on Pelagea Nilvna once again and bring her a few of our papers. *Vesovchikov grabs the papers.* The arrests have been very bad for our movement. Sidor and Pavel, for example, are the only ones who know many of the addresses of the peasants who want to read our newspaper.

VLASOVA: I understand. We've talked a lot too about the need to speak to the peasants.

VESOVCHIKOV: You would be needing to speak to a lot of people too. 120 million peasants, you couldn't do it. Revolution of any kind isn't possible in this country with people like that. The Russian will never make a revolution. It's more a thing for the West. The Germans now, they're revolutionaries, they'll make a revolution.

IVAN: We've heard from several provinces that the peasants are already destroying estate farms and appropriating estate land. They've confiscated grain and other provisions from the owners and they're distributing them to the starving. The peasants are on the move.

VESOVCHIKOV: Yes, but what does that mean? *To Pelagea Vlasova*: Just read what the progressive writers of the last century wrote about the psychology of the Russian peasant.

VLASOVA: I'd like to. I was able to read the report on the third party conference just recently, thanks to Nikolai Ivanovitch's classes in reading and writing.

VESOVCHIKOV: That's just another of your Lenin's mad ideas, trying to convince the proletariat it can take over the leadership of the revolution. It's doctrines like that which will destroy the last particle of the possibility of a revolution taking place. They simply make the progressive bourgeoisie afraid of making a revolution.

IVAN: What do you think, Pelagea Nilvona?

VLASOVA: Leading is very difficult. Even Sigorski the metal-worker makes life difficult for me with his pig-headedness, and you can't prove anything at all to educated people.

VESOVCHIKOV: Couldn't you write your newspaper in a slightly more entertaining way? No one's going to read that.

VLASOVA: We don't read it for entertainment, Nikolai Ivanovitch.

Ivan laughs.

VESOVCHIKOV: What's the matter?

IVAN: What've you done with your pretty picture of the Tsar? The room looks quite bare without it.

VESOVCHIKOV: I thought I'd take it down for a while. It gets boring having it in front of you all the time. By the way, why is there nothing in your newspapers about conditions in schools?

IVAN: I just thought — you can't have put that picture away just because it was boring, surely?

VLASOVA: Don't say that! Nikolai Ivanovitch is always looking for something new.

IVAN: I see.

VESOVCHIKOV: At all events, I don't like to see myself being treated like an idiot. I asked you something in connection with your newspaper.

IVAN: Nikolai, I can't remember anything ever changing in your flat. The frame alone cost 12 roubles.

VESOVCHIKOV: In that case I can hang the frame back up again, can't I. You've always taken me for a fool, which is why you're a fool yourself.

IVAN: Nikolai, I'm surprised. Your inflammatory talk and your scornful attitude towards our Tsar amaze me. You seem to have become an agitor. You've developed such a determined stare too. It's downright dangerous just to look at you.

VLASOVA: Stop annoying your brother! He's a very sensible person. I made him think again about the Tsar's Bloody Sunday. And since a lot of children learn things from him, it's very important what he says about things. Besides, he taught us reading and writing.

IVAN: I hope, as you taught them to read and write, you learnt something yourself.

VESOVCHIKOV: No. I learned absolutely nothing. These little people still understand very little about Marxism. I don't want to offend you, Mrs Vlasova. It's a very complicated subject of course, and for an untrained mind totally incomprehensible. The extraordinary thing about it is that it's the people who'll never understand it who gulp it down like hot cakes. Marxism in itself is not a bad thing. It even has much in its favour, though there are large holes in it of course, and Marx on many key issues sees the whole thing in completely the wrong light. There are all kinds of things I could say on the subject. Of course economics are important, but it's not only economics that are important. They are *also* important. What about sociology? I imagine biology could be just as important too. Where, I ask is human nature in this doctrine? Man will always remain true to his nature.

VLASOVA, *to Ivan*: But he's changed quite a bit, hasn't he.

Ivan takes his leave.

IVAN: Mrs Vlasova, I don't recognise my brother any more.

7. PELAGEA VLASOVA VISITS HER SON IN PRISON

Prison.

VLASOVA: The warden'll be keeping a close watch, but I've still got to find out the addresses of the peasants who used to ask for our newspaper. I only hope I can keep all the names in my head.

The warden brings Pavel in.

Pavel!

PAVEL: How are you, Mum?

WARDEN: You have to sit so there's space between you. There and there. Political conversation is not allowed.

PAVEL: In that case, tell me about home, Mother.

VLASOVA: Yes, Pavel.

PAVEL: Have you got a place to live?

VLASOVA: At Vesovchikov's, the teacher.

PAVEL: They look after you all right?

VLASOVA: Yes. But how are you?

PAVEL: I was worried whether they'd be able to support you sufficiently.

VLASOVA: Your beard's got thick.

PAVEL: Yes. Makes me look older, doesn't it.

VLASOVA: I went to Smilgin's funeral, you know. The police let fly again and arrested a few people. We were all there

WARDEN: That's politics, Mrs Vlasova!

VLASOVA: Oh? Really? It's hard to know what you *can* talk about.

WARDEN: In that case your visits are a waste of time. You've got nothing to talk about, but you still come running in here disturbing us. Remember: I'm held responsible.

PAVEL: Are you helping out around the house?

VLASOVA: That too. Vesovchikov and me are thinking of going out to the country next week.

PAVEL: The teacher?

VLASOVA: No.

PAVEL: You thinking of having a rest?

VLASOVA: Yes. *Quiet*. We need the addresses. *Loud*. Oh Pavel, we all miss you so much.

PAVEL, *quiet*: I swallowed the addresses when I got arrested. I just know one or two by heart.

VLASOVA: Oh Pavel, I'd never have thought I'd see my days out like this.

PAVEL, *quiet*: Lushin in Pirogovo.

VLASOVA, *quiet*: And in Krapivna? *Loud*. Really, you worry me so much!

PAVEL, *quiet*: Sulinovski.

VLASOVA: I pray for you too. *Quiet*. Sulinovski in Krapivna. *Loud*. I spend my evenings sitting on my own, by the lamp.

PAVEL, *quiet*: Terek in Tobraya.

VLASOVA: And Vesovchikov the teacher complains if I have noisy company.

PAVEL, *quiet*: And the rest of the addresses you can get from them.

WARDEN: Time's up.

VLASOVA: One more minute please, sir. I'm so confused. Ah Pavel, what's left for us old folk but to creep away so people don't have to see us any more. We're no good for anything any more. *Quiet*. Lushin in Pirogovo. *Loud*. People let us know our days are over. We've got nothing to look forward to. Everything we know belongs to the past. *Quiet*. Sulinovski in Tobraya. *Pavel shakes his head*. In Krapivna. *Loud*. And our experiences don't count for anything any more. Our advice does more harm than good, because between us and our sons is an unbridgeable gap. *Quiet*. Terek in Tobraya. *Loud*. We go one way and you go the other. *Quiet*. Terek in Tobraya. We've got nothing in common. The times to come are yours.

WARDEN: Visiting-time, though is over!

PAVEL, *bows*: Farewell, Mother.

VLASOVA, *bows too*: Farewell, Pavel.

SONG, *sung by the actor playing Pavel.*

They've got all their law-books and their regulations
They've got all their prisons and fortresses
(All their welfare institutions don't really count!)
They've got all their prison guards and judges
Who are overpaid and far too keen to oblige them
Well, why's that then?
Do they really think they'll wear us down with all that?
    Before they vanish, and that will be soon
        They will surely notice that all that cannot help them any
                                                            more.

They've got their newspapers and printing-presses
With which to attack us and silence our voices
(All their statesmen we don't need to count!)
They've got their parsons and their professors
Who are overpaid and far too keen to oblige them
Well, why's that then?
Is it because the truth's so frightening?
    Before they vanish, and that will be soon
'   They will surely notice that all that cannot help them any
                                                            more.

They've got their tanks and their cannon
Their machine-guns and their hand-grenades
(Their rubber truncheons don't really count!)
Their policemen and their soldiers
Who are underpaid but far too keen to oblige them.
Well, why's that then?
Is it because their enemy's so powerful?

They think they must find some support soon
To halt their imminent fall
One fine day though, and that will be soon
They'll come to see that that's no good to them at all.
They can shout out then all they want 'Stop now!'
Neither money nor cannon will answer their call!

8. IN THE SUMMER OF 1905 THE COUNTRY WAS SHAKEN BY PEASANT UPRISINGS AND AGRICULTURAL STRIKES.

a. Country road.

Pelagea Vlasova, who is approaching accompanied by two workers, is greeted by a shower of thrown stones. Her companions run off.

VLASOVA, *with a large lump on her forehead, to the stone-throwers*: Why are you throwing stones at us?

LUSHIN: Because you're strike-breakers.

VLASOVA: Oh, I see, we're strike-breakers, are we? That's why we're in such a hurry! Where's the strike, then?

LUSHIN: On the Smirnov estate.

VLASOVA: And you're the strikers? I can tell that from this lump. Only I'm not a strike-breaker. I've come from Rostov and I want to speak to a labourer on the estate. His name's Yegor Lushin.

LUSHIN: I'm Lushin.

VLASOVA: Pelagea Vlasova.

LUSHIN: Are you the woman people round here call 'The Mother'?

VLASOVA: Yes. I've brought our papers for you. We didn't know you were on strike, but I can see you're carrying on a hard fight. *She hands the papers over to Lushin.*

LUSHIN: I'm sorry we gave you that lump. Our strike's not going well. Strike-breakers came with you from town and tomorrow we're expecting more. We've got nothing to eat, but for them the estate butcher's already slaughtering pigs and calves.

There look. Can you see the estate kitchen chimney smoking for the strike-breakers?

VLASOVA: It's really a shame.

LUSHIN: The estate butcher's, the estate baker's and the estate dairy, of course, aren't on strike.

VLASOVA: Why not? Have you talked to them?

LUSHIN: There's no point. Why should they strike? They only cut us labourers' wages this time.

VLASOVA: Give me back the papers. *She divides the bundle of newspapers into two parts and gives him only half.*

LUSHIN: What about those? Why aren't you giving us all of them?

VLASOVA: These are going to the estate butcher's, the estate baker's and the estate dairy. There's workers there too, don't forget. We've got to talk to them. Where there's a worker, there's a way.

LUSHIN: Save yourself the trouble! *He goes.*

VLASOVA: That's how we carve each other up' worker against worker, and the exploiters laugh at us.

b. Estate kitchen.

Two strike-breakers sit eating and talk to the estate butcher.

1ST STRIKEBREAKER, *chewing, to the other*: The man who lets his country down in its hour of danger is a bastard. And the worker who strikes is letting his country down.

BUTCHER, *chopping meat*: How d'you mean, his country?

2ND STRIKEBREAKER: They're Russians and this is Russia. And Russia belongs to the Russians.

BUTCHER: You don't say.

2ND STRIKEBREAKER: Dead right. If man can't feel that — this meat's not quite done — there's no explaining it to him. You can smash his head in, though.

BUTCHER: Right!

1ST STRIKEBREAKER: This table's the fatherland. This meat's the fatherland.

BUTCHER: Only it's not quite done.

2ND STRIKEBREAKER: This seat I'm sitting in's the fatherland. And you, look – *to the butcher* – you're a piece of the fatherland too.

BUTCHER: Only I'm not quite done either.

1ST STRIKEBREAKER: It's every man's duty to defend his fatherland.

BUTCHER: Yeh, if it *is* his!

2ND STRIKEBREAKER: That's just your low-minded materialism.

BUTCHER: Arsehole!

The butcher's wife brings in Pelagea Vlasova, who is exaggerating the wound in her head.

WIFE: You sit down here. I'll make you a cold compress and then you must have something to eat to help you get over your shock. *To the others.* They threw a stone at her.

1ST STRIKEBREAKER: Yeh, that's the woman. She came down on the train with us.

2ND STRIKEBREAKER: The strikers did that to her. We were worried sick for her.

WIFE: Is it getting any better?

Vlasova nods.

2ND STRIKEBREAKER: Thank God.

WIFE: They fight like animals, just for a little bit of work. Look at that lump! *She goes to fetch water.*

VLASOVA, *to the audience*: How much more sympathy a lump arouses from people expecting lumps than from people handing them out!

1ST STRIKEBREAKER, *points with his fork to Vlasova*: This Russian woman was pelted with stones by Russian workers. Are you a mother?

VLASOVA: Yes.

1ST STRIKEBREAKER: A Russian mother pelted with stones!

BUTCHER: Yeh, and Russian ones too! *To the audience:* And I'm supposed to serve this trash my best soup. *To Vlasova:* Why'd they throw those things at you, then?

VLASOVA, *cooling her lump with a damp cloth*: They saw me walking along together with the strikebreakers.

2ND STRIKEBREAKER: The bastards!

VLASOVA: How come they're bastards? I was only thinking to myself just now, perhaps they're not bastards at all.

WIFE: Why'd they throw stones at you, then?

VLASOVA: Because they thought I was a bastard.

WIFE: How could they think you were a bastard?

VLASOVA: Because they thought I was a strike-breaker.

BUTCHER, *smiles*: So you think it's all right to throw stones at strike-breakers?

VLASOVA: Yes, of course.

BUTCHER, *beaming, to his wife*: Give her something to eat! Give her something to eat this minute! Give her two helpings! *He steps up to Vlasova*. My name's Vasil Yefimovitch. *Calling to his wife*. And bring the staff in! They can learn something here.

The staff appear in the doorway.

BUTCHER: This woman had stones thrown at her by strikers. She's got a lump on her head. Look, there it is. So I ask her: 'Why've you got that lump?' She says: 'Because they thought I was a strike-breaker.' I ask her: 'Should people throw stones at strike-breakers then?' And what does she say?

VLASOVA: Yes.

BUTCHER: My friends, when I heard that, I said: 'Give her something to eat. Give her two helpings! *To Vlasova*: Why aren't you eating, then? Is it too hot for you? *To wife*: Do you have to serve the food up boiling hot? D'you want her to burn her mouth?

VLASOVA, *pushes the plate away*: No, Vasil Yefimovitch, the food isn't too hot.

BUTCHER: Why aren't you eating then?

VLASOVA: Because this was cooked for the strikebreakers.

BUTCHER: Who's it cooked for?

VLASOVA; The strike-breakers.

BUTCHER: I see! That's interesting. So I'm a bastard too? You see that? I'm a bastard. And why am I a bastard? Because I'm supporting the strike-breakers. *To Vlasova*: Is that right? *He sits down next to her.* Isn't striking wrong, though? You'd say it depends what people are striking for. *Vlasova nods.* You'd say people's wages were being cut. But why shouldn't their wages be cut? Look around. Everything you see here belongs to Mr Smirnov, who lives in Odessa. Why shouldn't he cut our wages? *As the strike-breakers agree with him heartily*. It's his money, isn't it? So you don't think he should let the wage be two roubles one day and two kopecks the next? So you don't think he should? What happened last year, then? Even my wages got cut then. And what did I do — *To his wife* — on your advice? Nothing! And what's going to happen in September? I'll get cut again! And what am I making myself guilty of now? Of treason against the people who are also getting cut and who aren't putting up with it. So what am I? *To Vlasova*: So you won't eat my food. That's all I've been waiting for: one decent person to say to my face that she as a decent person won't eat my food. Now the cup's full. It's been full a long time in fact. It just needed one drop. — *He points to Vlasova* — to make it overflow. Anger and discontent aren't enough. A thing like this has got to have practical consequences. *To the strike-breakers*: Tell your Mister Smirnov he'll have to have his food sent out from Odessa. Best of all, he can cook it for himself, the pig.

WIFE: Don't get so excited.

BUTCHER: It wasn't for nothing I used to cook in factory canteens. I left because crap management didn't suit me. *As his wife tries to calm him down.* I thought, I'll go to the country, it's decent there. And what do I find? Another crap-hole, where I'm supposed to stuff strike-breakers full.

WIFE: We can always move on again.

BUTCHER: Dead right, we're leaving. *Grandly*. Bring in the pot of lentils. And you, fetch all the bacon. Whatever's hanging about. What's it been cooked for, after all?

WIFE: You'll only make yourself miserable. You'll ruin us yet.

BUTCHER, *to the strike-breakers*: Out of it, you saviours of the fatherland! We're striking. The kitchen-staff is on strike. Out! *He drives the strike-breakers out.* As a butcher I'm used to being the one to laugh last, and not the pig. *With his arm round*

his wife's shoulder, he steps up to Vlasova. Now go out and tell
the men who threw stones at you their soup's waiting for
them.

IN PRAISE OF VLASOVA, *recited by the estate builder and his
people*

> This is our comrade Vlasova, a good fighter
> Hard-working, cunning and reliable.
> Reliable in struggle, cunning against our enemy and hard-
> working
> In her agitation. Her work is small
> Carried our with a will and indispensable.
> She's not alone, wherever she fights.
> Others like her fight cunningly, reliably and with a will
> In Twer, Glasgow, Lyons and Chicago
> Shanghai and Calcutta
> Vlasovas of all countries, good little moles
> Unknown soldiers of the revolution
> Indispensable.

9. 1912. PAVEL RETURNS FROM EXILE IN SIBERIA.

Teacher Vesovchikov's flat.

*Vlasova, Vasil Yefimovitch and a young worker carry a printing-
press into the teacher Vesovchikov's flat.*

VESOVCHIKOV: Pelagea Vlasova, you can't set up a printing-
press here in my home. You're abusing my sympathy for the
movement. You know that theoretically I share the same
ground as you, but this is going much too far.

VLASOVA: Do I understand you right, Nikolai Ivanovitch?
You're for our leaflets — I remind you that you drew up the
last one for the Workers Commune yourself — but you're
against their being printed?

They set up the machine.

VESOVCHIKOV: No. But printing them here, that's what I'm
against.

VLASOVA, *hurt*: We'll bear that in mind, Nikolai Ivanovitch.

They work on.

VESOVCHIKOV: And then what?

WORKER: Once Mrs Vlasova's got a thing in her head, there's nothing you can do. We've already had considerable difficulty with her in the past in that respect. No one'll notice anything anyway.

VLASOVA: The reason we've got to print more papers now is because they keep confiscating them from us.

Vesovchikov goes into the next room and reads. They start printing. The machine makes a lot of noise. Vesovchikov rushes in.

It's a bit loud, isn't it.

VESOVCHIKOV: The lamp's falling off the wall in my room! I'm afraid your printing illegal publications here is quite impossible, if its going to make such a noise.

VLASOVA: Nikolai Ivanovitch, we noticed ourselves that the machine was a bit loud.

YEFIMOVITCH: If we had something to put underneath it, you wouldn't be able to hear a thing in the flats next door. Have you got something to put underneath it, Nikolai Ivanovitch?

VESOVCHIKOV: No, nothing at all.

VLASOVA: Not so loud! The lady next door showed me a piece of felt she brought to make coats for her children. I'll go and ask her for it. Don't do any more printing till I come back. *She goes next door.*

YEFIMOVITCH, *to Vesovchikov*: Nikolai Ivanovitch, we're sorry if she's upset you.

WORKER: In fact we brought her here so she'd have a rest from politics. We'd never have set up an illegal press here ourselves, would we, Vasil Yefimovitch? But she wouldn't have it any other way, you see.

VESOVCHIKOV: I'm very cross. For example, I also disapprove most strongly of your continuing to take money from her. Recently I came home and was forced to look on as she stood there with her old purse fishing out her few kopecks membership dues.

YEFIMOVITCH: Yes, but we don't get anything for nothing. The revolution is directed against poverty. But even then it costs money. The Mother's very strict about collecting dues. That's another half a loaf we've got to go without, she says, for the sake of the cause. Our firm's got to go places, she says when she's collecting them in.

A knock. They hide the machine. Vesovchikov opens the door.

PAVEL'S VOICE, *outside*: Does Pelagea Vlasova live here? My name's Pavel Vlasov.

VESOVCHIKOV: Her son!

PAVEL, *comes in*: Good day.

EVERYONE: Good day.

PAVEL: Where's my mother, then?

VESOVCHIKOV: Next door.

YEFIMOVITCH: She'll be back in a minute. Your mother told us you were . . .

PAVEL: Away for a while!

YEFIMOVITCH, *laughs*: Yes.

They hear Vlasova coming back.

VESOVCHIKOV: Sit over here. Let's make it a real surprise for your mother.

They make Pavel sit on a chair oppostie the door and arrange themselves around him. Vlasova comes in.

VLASOVA: Pavel! *She embraces him*. He gets thinner and thinner! Instead of fatter, he gets thinner! I didn't think they'd be able to hold you for long. How did you get away from them? How long can you stay here?

PAVEL: I've got to move on this evening.

VLASOVA: You can still take your coat off, though, can't you?

Pavel takes his coat off.

VESOVCHIKOV: I heard your aim was to fight for freedom, but in the process you set up in your party the very worst kind of slavery. Some freedom! Nothing but orders and compulsion!

VLASOVA: Look here, Nikolai Ivanovitch, this is the way it is: we're not as much against those orders as you are. We've got a more urgent need for them. We're taking on more — and don't take this the wrong way — than you. It's the same with

freedom as it is with your money, Nikolai Ivanovitch. Since
I've only been giving you a little pocket-money, you're able
to buy yourself a lot more. By spending less money for a
while, you can then spend more money. You can't argue with
that.

VESOVCHIKOV: I shall give up arguing with you. You're a
terrible tyrant.

VLASOVA: Yes, well, we have to be, don't we.

YEFIMOVITCH: Did you get the felt? *To Pavel*: We've got to
have the paper ready by eight o'clock.

PAVEL: Get printing then.

VLASOVA, *beaming*: Start printing right away, so we'll have a
little more time later. What about this then: that Marfa
Alexandrovna turned my request down flat in my face. Her
reason: the felt was meant for coats for her children. I say:
'Marfa Alexandrovna, I saw your children coming out of school
only recently. In coats.' 'Coats,' she says, 'those aren't coats,
they're patched up rags. The other children at school laugh at
them.' 'Marfa Alexandrovna,' I say, 'poor people have bad coats.
Give me the felt, until tomorrow morning at least. I assure you
it'll be of more use to your children to give it to me than a
fancy coat would be.' She was so unreasonable though! She
actually didn't give it to me! Not for two kopecks of good
sense! *She takes a couple of pieces of felt from under her
apron and lays them under the machine.*

VESOVCHIKOV: What's that, then?

VLASOVA: The felt, of course!

They all laugh.

YEFIMOVITCH: Why d'you keep complaining about this Marfa
Alexandrovna woman so much, then?

VLASOVA: Because she forced me to steal the stuff. We've got to
have it after all. And it's very good for her children that papers
like this get printed. That's the honest truth!

YEFIMOVITCH: Pelagea Vlasova, in the name of the revolution
we thank you for the felt!

Laughter.

VLASOVA: I'll take it back round tomorrow. *To Pavel, who has
sat down*: D'you want some bread?

YEFIMOVITCH, *by the machine*: Who's going to take the finished pages out, if he does?

Vlasova stands by the machine. Pavel gets himself some bread.

VLASOVA: Look in the bin.

PAVEL: Don't worry about me. I even found a piece of bread in Siberia once.

VLASOVA: D'you hear that? He's accusing me. I don't look after him. At least I can slice that loaf for you.

VESOVCHIKOV: And who's going to take the finished pages out here?

PAVEL, *cuts himself a piece of bread from the loaf while the others print*: The pages will be taken out by the mother of the revolutionary Pavel Vlasov, the revolutionary Pelagea Vlasova. Does she look after him? No chance! Does she make him a cup of tea? Does she run his bath for him? Does she slaughter a calf? No chance! Fleeing from Siberia to Finland amind the icy blasts of the North Wind, the salvoes of the gendarmes in his ears, he finds no refuge where he can lay his head down, except in an illegal printing-shop. And his mother, instead of stroking his hair, takes the finished pages out!

VLASOVA: If you want to help us, come here. Andrei'll make room for you.

Pavel takes over the place opposite his mother at the printing machine. They recite:

VLASOVA: Things weren't bad for you, were they?

PAVEL: Everything was fine, except for the typhus.

VLASOVA: You've always eaten properly at least?

PAVEL: Until the times when I had nothing, yes.

VLASOVA: Look after yourself. Will you be away long?

PAVEL: If you work well here, no.

VLASOVA: Will you be working there too?

PAVEL: Definitely. And it's as important there as here.

There is a knock. Sigorski comes in.

SIGORSKI: Pavel, you've got to leave at once. Here's the ticket. Comrade Issay will be waiting for you at the station with the passport.

PAVEL: I thought it'd be a few hours at least. *He takes his coat.*

VLASOVA, *goes to get her coat*: I'll go down with you.

SIGORSKI: No, It'd be dangerous for Pavel. They know you, but they don't know him.

She helps him back into his coat.

PAVEL: Goodbye, Mother.

VLASOVA: Next time let's hope I can slice the bread for you.

PAVEL: Let's hope so. Goodbye, Comrades.

Pavel and Sigorski go.

VESOVCHIKOV: God will help him, Pelagea Vlasova.

VLASOVA: I don't know so much.

She turns back to the printing-maching. They print on. Vlasova recites:

IN PRAISE OF THE THIRD CAUSE

> Over and over you hear
> How mothers have sons who forsake them, but then I
> Held on to my son. How'd I keep my son? Through
> The third cause.
> For he and I were two, but the third
> Common cause that we followed bound us so close
> Together.
> I have often myself heard
> Sons speak with their parents.
> How much better we got on when we talked
> About the cause we shared, the third cause which bound us
> > as one
> Shared by so many, the great common cause that binds them.
> How close to each other we were, standing close to our
> Great cause! How good to each other we were
> Close to our great cause!

10. ATTEMPTING TO CROSS THE FINNISH BORDER, PAVEL VLASOV IS ARRESTED AND SHOT.

Vesovchikov's flat.

Vlasova sits in the kitchen, a letter in her hand.

CHORUS, *sung by the Revolutionary Workers to Vlasova:*

Comrade Vlasova, your son
Has been shot. But as
He made his way there, towards the wall of execution
He walked towards a wall made by his own fellow workers.
The very rifles that aimed at his heart and the bullets that
followed
Had been made by his fellow workers. Only they had all
departed
Or had all been driven, driven away, yet still for him were
present
And with him in the work of their hands. Not even
Those who shot at him were different from him, nor would
they always be unteachable either.
Granted, he still went out bound fast in irons, in irons
Forged by his comrades, and now used to shackle a comrade,
And though he understood, he could not see why.
And he saw how, from the roadway, the works packed to-
gether,
Chimney on chimney, and as it was morning now —
For they take them all out as a rule in the morning —
They were all bare, but he alone could see them filled
With that mighty army, that army which grew and grew
And grows on still.
But it was men just like him who were leading him out to the
wall
And though he understood, he could not see why.

Living-room. Three women come in, bringing a bible and a pot of food.

THE LANDLADY, *in the door*: We'll forget all our differences
with Mrs Vlasova, shall we, and sit down with her as Christians
and offer her our sympathy.

They come in.

Dear Mrs Vlasova, you are not alone in these trying times. The whole house feels for you.

Two of the women are overcome with emotion and sit down. They sob loudly.

VLASOVA, *after a pause*: Have some tea. It'll refresh you.

She brings them tea.

Are you feeling easier now?

THE LANDLADY: You're so composed, Mrs Vlasova.

HER NIECE FROM THE COUNTRY: You're quite right, though. We're all in God's hands.

THE POOR WOMAN: And God knows what He's doing.

Vlasova is silent.

We thought we'd take it on ourselves to look after you a bit. I expect you've not been feeding yourself properly these past few days. Here's a pot of food. All you have to do is warm it up. *She hands over the pot.*

VLASOVA: Thank you very much, Lydia Antonovna. It's very kind of you to have thought of it. And it's very kind of you all to come.

THE LANDLADY: Dear Vlasova, I've brought you a bible too, in case you should want something to read. You may keep it as long as you wish. *She gives Vlasova the bible.*

VLASOVA: Thank you for the kind thought, Vera Stepanovna. It's a beautiful book. Would you be very offended, though, if I gave it you back? When the teacher Vesovchikov went on holiday, he allowed me to use his books. *She gives the bible back.*

THE LANDLADY: I just thought you probably wouldn't want to be reading your political newspapers at this time.

THE NIECE: Do you really read them every day?

VLASOVA: Yes.

THE LANDLADY: Mrs Vlasova, my bible has often been a great comfort to me.

Silence.

THE POOR WOMAN: Don't you have any photographs of him?

VLASOVA: No. I had some. But then we destroyed them all, so the police wouldn't get hold of them.

THE POOR WOMAN: It's nice to have something for memory's sake though.

NIECE: They say he was such a good-looking young man too!

VLASOVA: I remember now, I have got a photograph. It's a wanted notice. He cut it out of a paper for me.

The women look at the wanted notice.

THE LANDLADY: Mrs Vlasova, it's down here in black and white. Your son was a criminal. He had no faith, and you yourself have never made any secret of it — I'd even say you've taken every opportunity to let us know what you think of our faith.

VLASOVA: That's right, Vera Stepanovna. Nothing.

THE LANDLADY: And even now you've not come to any other conclusion?

VLASOVA: No, Vera Stepanovna.

THE LANDLADY: So you're still of the opinion that man can do everything by reason alone?

THE POOR WOMAN: I told you I was sure Mrs Vlasova wouldn't have changed her mind, Vera Stepanovna.

THE LANDLADY: But I heard you weeping only the other night — through the wall, you know.

VLASOVA: I'm sorry.

THE LANDLADY: There's no need to be sorry. That wasn't the way I meant it, of course. But tell me, was that weeping rational?

VLASOVA: No.

THE LANDLADY: There, you see, that's how far reason gets you.

VLASOVA: My weeping wasn't rational. But when I stopped, my stopping was rational. What Pavel did was good.

THE LANDLADY: Why was he shot then?

THE POOR WOMAN: Everyone was against him, weren't they?

VLASOVA: Yes, but by being against him, they were against themselves.

THE LANDLADY: Mrs Vlasova, mankind needs God. <u>Against Fate we are powerless.</u>

VLASOVA: We say: man is his own fate.

NIECE: Dear Mrs Vlasova, we in the country . . .

THE LANDLADY, *points to her*: My niece — she's just on a visit here.

NIECE: We in the country see these things differently. You folk here don't have seed lying in the fields, just the loaf in the cupboard. You only see the milk, you don't see the cow. You don't have a sleepless night when there's storms in the sky. And what's hail to you?

VLASOVA: I see, and in situations like that you pray to God?

NIECE: Yes.

VLASOVA: And in spring you go on processions and pilgrimages.

NIECE: Right.

VLASOVA: And then the storms come and then it hails. And the cow gets sick anyway. Haven't the farmers in your region got some kind of insurance against a bad harvest or cattle diseases yet? Insurance can help when praying hasn't helped at all. So you don't need to pray to God any more when there are storms in the sky, but you do have to be insured. It'll help you, you see. If he's that unimportant, that's bad for God. But then the hope is that once this God has disappeared from your fields, he might disappear from your heads too. In my youth everyone still believed firmly he sat somewhere in heaven, looking like an old man. Then came aeroplanes, and it said in the newspapers that even in the heavens everything was now measurable. No one talked any more about a God sitting in heaven. Instead of that you then often heard the view he was like a sort of gas, nowhere and yet everywhere. But when you then read about all the different things gases were composed of. God wasn't amongst them, so he couldn't even remain a gas because people knew them all. So he just got thinner and thinner till he vanished into thin air, so to speak. From time to time you read these days that all he is really is a spiritual symbol, but that's very suspect, isn't it.

THE POOR WOMAN: So you think because people don't notice him any more, he's no longer so important.

THE LANDLADY: Mrs Vlasova, don't forget why God took your Pavel away from you.

VLASOVA: It was the Tsar who took him from me, and I haven't forgotten why either.

THE LANDLADY: God took him, not the Tsar.

VLASOVA, *to the poor woman*: Lydia Antonovna, I hear that God, who took my Pavel from me, is currently planning to take your room away from you next Saturday. Is that true? God gave you notice?

THE LANDLADY: I gave her notice because she's failed to pay her rent three times now.

VLASOVA: So when God ordained you shouldn't get your three weeks' rent, Vera Stepanovna, what did you do?

Vera Stepanovna is silent.

You threw Lydia Antonovna out on the street. And you, Lydia Antonovna, what did you do when God ordained you should be thrown out on the street? I'd advise you to ask the landlady to lend you her bible. Then when you're sitting out in the street in the cold, you can leaf through it and read from it to your children that man must fear God.

THE LANDLADY: If you'd read to your son from the bible more, he'd still be living today.

VLASOVA: But very badly, he'd be living very badly. Why are you people so afraid of death? My son wasn't all that afraid of death. *She recites*:

He was very alarmed though, at the misery
In our cities, apparent to every eye.
It's the hunger appals us, the degradation
Of those who feel it and those who cause it.
Don't be afraid of death so much as an inadequate life.
Pause. What good does it do you to fear God, Lydia Antonovna?
You'd be better off fearing Vera Stepanovna. Just as it wasn't the unfathomable law of God that snatched my son Pavel away, but the fathomable law of the Tsar, so Vera Stepanovna has thrown you out in the street because a man who lives in a villa and has nothing godlike about him at all has chased you away from your place of work. Why talk about God? That there are many mansions in 'our Father's house' they tell you; but there are too few flats in Rostov and why, that they don't tell you.

THE POOR WOMAN: Give me the bible a moment, Vera Stepanovna. In the bible it says quite clearly: Love Thy Neighbour. So why are you throwing me out on the street? Give me the bible, I'll find the page for you. It stands to reason they shot Pavel Vlasov. He was for the workers and a worker himself. *She grabs the bible.* Give me the book, I'll show you the page . . .

THE LANDLADY: You won't get the bible from me for that purpose, not for that purpose.

THE POOR WOMAN: For what purpose, then? For no good one, I bet!

THE LANDLADY: That is the Word of God!

THE POOR WOMAN: That's just the point. Your God is of no use to me, if I can't see any sign of him! *She tries to tear the bible away from the landlady.*

THE LANDLADY: Now I'll find a passage for you, namely the one about laying hands on other people's property.

THE POOR WOMAN: I want the book.

THE LANDLADY, *holding on hard to the bible*. It's my property.

THE POOR WOMAN: Yes, like the whole house, you mean?

The bible is torn to shreds.

THE NIECE, *picks up the pieces of the bible*: Now it's torn.

VLASOVA, *who has put the pot of food in a safe place*: Better a torn-up bible than spilt food.

THE POOR WOMAN: If I didn't believe there was a God in heaven who requites everything, good and bad, I'd join Pelagea Vlasova's party today. *She goes.*

THE LANDLADY: Pelagea Vlasova, you see what you've done to Lydia Antonovna. It was because he spoke the way you are now you son was shot, and you deserve no better. Come.

She goes with her relative.

VLASOVA: You unhappy people! *She sits down, exhausted.* Pavel!

11.   THE DEATH OF HER SON AND THE YEARS OF THE STOLYPIN REACTION HAVE BROUGHT VLASOVA'S REVOLUTIONARY ACTIVITY TO A STANDSTILL. ON HER SICKBED SHE RECEIVES NEWS OF THE OUTBREAK OF WORLD WAR.

Vesovchikov's flat.

VESOVCHIKOV, *to the Doctor*: She hasn't been well since her son died. I don't mean her housework, but a quite particular job she always used to do, she doesn't do any more.

THE DOCTOR: She's completely exhausted and on no account should she get up. She's an old woman after all.

He goes. Vesovchikov goes into the kitchen and sits by Vlasova's bed.

VLASOVA: What's in the papers?

VESOVCHIKOV: The war's here.

VLASOVA: War? What are we doing?

VESOVCHIKOV: The Tsar's declared a state of siege. Of all the socialist parties only the Bolsheviks have spoken out against the war. Our five members in the Duma have already been arrested and packed off to Siberia for high treason.

VLASOVA: That's bad. — If the Tsar's mobilising, then we workers've got to mobilise too. — I've got to get up.

VESOVCHIKOV: On no account may you get up. You're ill. What can we do against the Tsar and all the potentates of Europe? I'll go down and buy the late extra edition. Now they'll annihilate the Party totally. *He goes.*

CHORUS, *sung by the Revolutionary Workers to Vlasova*

> Get up, for the Party is in danger!
> You are ill, but the Party's dying
> You are weak, but you must help us!
> Get up, for the Party is in danger!
>
> You who have doubted in us
> Doubt us no longer
> Our time has come now.
> You who have sometimes cursed the Party

Curse no more the Party which
They are destroying.

Get up, for the Party is in danger!
Up quickly!
You are ill, but we still need your help.
Don't die, you've got to help us.
Don't stay away, we're going into battle.
Get up, for the Party is in danger! Get up!

*During this chorus Pelagea Vlasova has got up with some difficulty,
dressed herself, picked up her bag and unsteadily, but walking
faster and faster, has crossed the room and gone out of the door.*

12. AGAINST THE STREAM.

Street corner.

*Several workers carry Vlasova, who has been bloodily beaten,
into a corner between two houses.*

1ST WORKER: What's wrong with her?

2ND WORKER: We saw this old woman in the middle of the
crowd cheering the troops off to war. Suddenly she shouted
out: 'Down with the war, long live the revolution!' Then the
police came up and beat her over the head with their
truncheons. We dragged her here between these houses quick.
Wash her face off for her then!

THE WORKERS: Come on, old girl, you'd better run now, or
they'll catch you again!

VLASOVA: Where's my bag?

THE WORKERS: It's here.

VLASOVA: Wait! I've got some pamphlets here in my bag.
There's something in them about the position of us workers in
the war: the truth.

THE WORKERS: Go home, old girl, leave the truth in your hand-
bag. It's dangerous. If they're found on us, we'll only get
locked up. Haven't you had enough yourself?

VLASOVA: No, no, you ought to know about it! It's not knowing that keeps us under.

THE WORKERS: And the police.

VLASOVA: They don't know either.

THE WORKERS: But our leaders tell us we've got to help beat the Germans first and defend our country.

VLASOVA, *recites:* What kind of leaders are those?
Side by side you fight with your class enemy
Worker against worker.
Your organisations, painfully built up
By denying yourself pennies, will be smashed to pieces.
Everything you've learned is forgotten
And the solidarity of all workers in all countries is forgotten.

THE WORKERS: None of that applies any more. We went on strike against the war in several factories. Our strikes were smashed. The revolution won't come now. Go home, old girl, see the world the way it is. What you want will never be. Never, never!

VLASOVA: Well, at least read what we've got to say about the situation, won't you? *She offers them the pamphlets.* You don't even want to read them?

THE WORKERS: We can see you mean well, but we don't want to take your pamphlets any more. We don't want to get ourselves into trouble any more.

VLASOVA: Ye-es, but remember: the whole world — *Shouting so that the terrified workers have to hold her mouth shut —* lives in a monstrous darkness, and until now you alone were the only ones who could still reached by reason. Think before you give up!

13.   1916 TIRELESSLY, THE BOLSHEVIKS FIGHT AGAINST THE IMPERIALIST WAR.

Patriotic copper collection centre.

Seven women carrying copper utensils stand lined up in front of a door decorated with a flag and the inscription: 'Patriotic copper collection centre.' Among them is Vlasova with a small beaker. An official in civilian clothes comes and opens the door.

OFFICIAL: It has just been announced that our brave troops, with exemplary and heroic courage and for the fourth time, have seized the fortress of Przemysl from the enemy. 100,000 dead, 2,000 prisoners. Army High Command have decreed that throughout Russia all schools be closed and bells rung. Long live our Holy Russia! Hurrah! Hurrah! Hurrah! The copper delivery counter will be open in five minutes. *He goes inside.*

VLASOVA: Hooray!

A WOMAN: That's really nice, our war going so well.

VLASOVA: I've only got this tiny little beaker, though. It'll only make five, six cartridges at the most. How many of those are going to hit anybody? Two out of six perhaps, and out of those two, one at most will be fatal. That kettle of yours must be twenty cartridges at least, and that jug that lady up front's got's a grenade even. A grenade can pick off five to six men in one go, just like that. *Counts the utensils.* One, two, three, four, five, six, seven — hang on, that lady's got two, hasn't she, so that's eight. Eight. Well, that's another small offensive mounted, isn't it. *She laughs gently.* I nearly didn't bring my little beaker here, you know. I meet these two soldiers on my way here — someone ought to report them really — they say to me: 'That's right, you old bag, give your copper in so the war'll never stop.' What about that, eh? Isn't that terrible? 'You ought to be shot,' I said. 'On the spot. If I was giving in my little beaker only so they could stop your dirty mouths with it, it wouldn't have been given in vain. It'd just about go to two cartridges. Because why am I, Pelagea Vlasova, giving in my copper beaker? I'm giving it in so the war won't end!'

WOMAN: What are you saying? The war won't end if we hand in our copper? That's exactly why we are handing it in, so it will end.

VLASOVA: No, we're handing it in, so it won't end.

A LADY DRESSED IN BLACK: No, if they've got copper and can make grenades out there, they'll win a lot quicker, won't they? Then the war'll stop!

VLASOVA: Ah no, if they've got grenades it stands to reason it won't stop, because then they can just keep going. As long as

they've got ammunition they'll carry on. They're giving it in on
the other side too, you know.

WOMAN, *points to a sign*: 'Give in your copper and shorten the
war.' Can't you read?

VLASOVA: Give in your copper and lengthen the war! It's for
spies, that stuff!

LADY IN BLACK: But why do you want the war to go on longer?

VLASOVA: 'Cos my son'll be a sergeant in six months' time.
Another two offensives and my son'll make sergeant. And then
he'll get twice the pay, won't he. And besides, we've got to get
Armenia yet, haven't we, and Galizia, and we really need Turkey.

LADY IN BLACK: What do we need?

VLASOVA: Turkey. And the money we borrowed from France,
that's got to be paid back too, hasn't it. In that sense it's a war
of liberation.

WOMAN: Naturally. Of course it's a war of liberation. But that's
no reason why it should last into eternity, is it?

VLASOVA: Yes, of course. Another six months at least.

LADY IN BLACK: And you think it'll last that long if they get
more copper?

VLASOVA: Yes, of course. The soldiers aren't fighting for nothing
after all. You've got someone out there too, have you?

LADY IN BLACK: Yes, my son.

VLASOVA: You see? You've got your son out there already, and
now you're giving your copper too. That way it'll go on
another six months for sure.

LADY IN BLACK: Now I don't know where I am at all. One
minute the word is the war'll get shorter, the next it'll get
longer. Which am I supposed to believe? I've lost my husband
already, and now my son's at Przemysl. I'm going home. *She goes.*

The bells start ringing.

WOMAN: Victory bells!

VLASOVA: Yes, we're winning! We give our little beakers away,
our kettles and our copper jugs, but we're winning! We've got
nothing left to eat, but we're winning! You're either for the Tsar
and his victory or you're against him. We're winning, but we've
also got to win! Or there'll be a revolution. That's certain. And

then what'll happen to our beloved Tsar? We've got to stand by him in times like these. Look at the Germans. They're already eating the leaves off the trees for their Kaiser!

WOMAN: What are you talking about exactly? Only a minute ago a woman here took her kettle and ran away, and all because of you.

A WOMAN WORKER: You shouldn't have gone and told her that, you up the front there, about wanting the war to go on longer. No one else wants that, do they?

VLASOVA: What? What about the Tsar? And the generals? D'you think they're afraid of war with the Germans? What they say is: Keep on at the enemy! Victory or death! And that's right. Can't you hear the bells? You only hear them at victories and funerals. Why are you against the war anyway? Who are you in any case? We here are a cut above the rest, If I'm not mistaken. You're a working woman, aren't you? Are you a working woman or not? Go on, admit it! You chuck yourself in here with the rest of us! Don't forget there's still a difference between people like you and us!

A GIRL IN SERVICE: You shouldn't say that to her. She's giving up her things for the fatherland too.

VLASOVA, *to the working woman*: Rubbish. You can't be standing there whole-heartedly, can you. What use is the war to you? It's pure hypocrisy, you standing there isn't it. We can get along quite well without you and your kind. This is our war! No one objects if you workers want to join in, but that doesn't mean you've been with us that long. You go back to your factory and see you get a better wage and don't come pushing in here where you don't belong. *To the girl in service*: You can take her old lumber from her, if she absolutely has to hand it in.

The working woman goes away, angry.

THIRD WOMAN: Who is that anyway, shooting her mouth off down there?

FOURTH WOMAN: I've been listening to her drive people away for the last half-hour now!

SECOND WOMAN: D'you know what she is? She's a Bolshevik!

WOMEN: What? D'you think she is? — She's a Bolshevik! And a very clever one at that! — Don't get involved with her, take no

notice of her. — Beware of Bolshevism, it has a thousand faces!
— As soon as a policeman comes along, she'll be led off!

VLASOVA, *leaves the queue*: Yes, I'm a Bolshevik! But you're
murderesses, standing there! No animal would give up its
young the way you have yours: without sense and
understanding, for a bad cause. You deserve to have the wombs
torn out of you, they should dry up and you become sterile
where you stand. Your sons don't need to come back. To
mothers like you? Shooting for a bad cause, they should be sho
for a bad cause. But you are the murderesses.

FIRST WOMAN, *turns round*: I'll show you what you deserve,
you Bolshevik!

OFFICIAL: The copper delivery counter is open.

*The woman advances on Vlasova with her jug in her hand and hits
her in the face. Another turns round too and spits in front of her.
Then the three women go in.*

GIRL IN SERVICE: Don't take it to heart. Tell me what I'm to do
though. I know you Bolsheviks are against the war, but I'm in
service. I can't go back to my master and mistress with these
copper jugs. can I. I don't want to hand them in, but if I don't,
I shan't have been of use to anybody and I'll be dismissed.
So what should I do?

VLASOVA: You can't do anything on your own. Hand the copper
kettles in in your master's name. In the name of your master
people like you will be making ammunition from them. And
people like you will shoot with it. But against that, people
like you will decide at whom! Come this evening to — *She
whispers the address in her ear*. A worker from the Putilov
plant will be speaking there, and we can explain to you what
you should do, Only don't tell anyone the address who shouldn't
know it.

14. 1917. AMID THE RANKS OF STRIKING WORKERS AND MUTINYING SOLDIERS MARCHES PELAGEA VLASOVA, 'THE MOTHER'.

Street.

IVAN: As we crossed the Lubin Prospekt we were already many thousand. Something like fifty factories were on strike, and the strikers joined our ranks to demonstrate against the war and Tsarist domination.

YEFIMOVITCH: In the winter of 1916–7, 250,000 men struck in the factories.

GIRL IN SERVICE: We carried banners with the inscription 'Down with the War! Long live the Revolution!' and red flags. A sixty-year-old woman carries our flag. We said to her: 'The flag isn't too heavy for you, is it? Give us the flag.' She, however, said:

VLASOVA: No. I'll give you it when I'm tired, then you can carry it. For I, Pelagea Vlasova, a worker's widow and a worker's mother, still have a lot of things to do. When I saw with sorrow many years ago how my son no longer ate his fill, at first all I did was whine. So nothing changed. Then I helped him in his fight for the kopeck. In those days we used to take part in small strikes for better wages. Now we're taking part in a huge strike in the ammunition factories and fighting for power in the state.

GIRL IN SERVICE: A lot of people say that what we want will never happen. We ought to be satisfied with what we have. The power of the ruling class is secure. We would always be beaten down, again and again. Even a lot of workers say: 'It'll never happen.'

VLASOVA, *recites*:

> While you're alive, don't say never!
> Security isn't certain
> And things won't stay as they are.
> When the ruling class has finished speaking
> Those they ruled will have their answer.
> Who dares to answer never?
> On whom is the blame if their oppression stays? On us!
> On whom does it fall to destroy it? On us!
> So if you are beaten down, you just rise again!
> If you think you've lost, fight on!

Once you have seen where you stand, there is nothing can
hold you back again.
For those defeated today will be the victors tomorrow
And from 'never' comes our 'today'.

2084